Contemporary Crafts

Decoupage

JULIET MOXLEY

Contemporary Crafts

Decoupage

JULIET MOXLEY

An Owl Book

HENRY HOLT
AND
COMPANY

NEW YORK

To Jill Sheridan
on being 40

Henry Holt and Company, Inc.
Publishers since 1866
115 West 18th Street
New York, New York 10011

Henry Holt® is a registered trademark
of Henry Holt and Company, Inc.

Library of Congress Catalog Card Number: 93-79500

ISBN 0-8050-2813-7

Henry Holt books are available for special
promotions and premiums. For details contact:
Director, Special Markets.

First American/Owl Book Edition — 1994

Designed and edited by
Anness Publishing Limited, London

Editorial Director: Joanna Lorenz
Project Editor: Penelope Cream
Design: Millions Design
Photographer: John Freeman
Assisted by: Maria Ortia
Illustrator: Paula Soper

Printed and bound in Spain by
Printer industria grafica s.a.

1   3   5   7   9   10   8   6   4   2

PUBLISHERS' NOTE

*The author and publishers have made every effort to ensure
that all instructions contained within this book are accurate
and safe, and cannot accept liability for any resulting injury,
damage or loss to persons or property however it may arise.*
*Although photocopying is suggested as a means of
reproducing images, the author and publishers advise readers
to take careful note of the photocopying and copyright
reproduction laws.*

CONTENTS

INTRODUCTION	7
MATERIALS AND EQUIPMENT	10
BASIC TECHNIQUES	14
GALLERY	16
PROJECTS	
VICTORIAN TRAY	27
HEART BOXES	33
HAT BOX	37
DRESSING ROOM SCREEN	41
KITCHEN CHAIR	47
FLORAL MIRROR	51
CELESTIAL CLOCK	57
DECOUPAGE TIN	61
CIRCUS FRIEZE	65
JEWELLERY BOX	69
WASTE-PAPER BASKET	73
DUMMY BOARD	79
GOLDEN FLOWER BOWL	83
BATHROOM TILES	87
MUSIC CUPBOARD	91
SUPPLIERS	95
INDEX	96

INTRODUCTION

The word 'decoupage' comes from the French verb *découper*, to cut out. In French, the word refers to cutting and stamping out leather, but in English it has come to mean the art of decorating surfaces with paper cut-outs. The process is amazingly simple: illustrations and prints are chosen, cut out and arranged in a new design on an object, then stuck down and varnished or lacquered.

Paper cut-outs have been used in European folk art since the introduction of paper in the 12th and 13th centuries, but decoupage as we know it is thought to have started in Italy in the late 17th century. The art spread to France as *l'art scriban*; the term is thought to have originated via a traveller who saw a desk decorated with decoupage and mistakenly thought the term *scriban* applied to the decoration rather than the desk. It was popular among the ladies of the court of Louis XIV, who would cut out original drawings and prints while they sat in their salons. The most popular motifs were a combination of lace edgings, dainty flowers, cherubs and butterflies. Lithographs, block prints and etchings were all used and the works of Boucher, Huet, Watteau and Jean Baptiste Pillement were reproduced specifically for this purpose. Pillement's designs were especially sought-after, and his witty drawings of dancing Chinese figures, fragile bridges and exotic trees were used to decorate everything from walls, spinets, desks and screens, to boxes

. . . .

These elegant hat boxes, decorated by Emma Whitfield, incorporate recurring themes. The method for the decoupage on the large hat box in the foreground is on page 37.

and trinkets. His popularity spread outside France into the rest of Europe, and copies of his work are still used by decoupers today to recreate an 18th-century style.

In Britain a form of decoupage known as japanning evolved from a thriving papier mâché industry. Japanning emulated the lacquer work of the Japanese, and was applied to wood, leather, tin and papier mâché. Many of the designs were in fact Chinese, but the quality of Japanese lacquer work was considered superior, and so the name was adopted for the whole process, including the applied motifs. The popularity of japanning in England was so great that a *Ladies*

. . . .

Gerry Copp's papier mâché bowls are decorated in an unusual form of decoupage; hand-made recycled papers of bright, contrasting shades are laid down in collage form, creating the patterns as they overlap.

Amusement Book was published in 1780, containing 1500 prints which were suitable for decoupage, tapestry design and ceramics.

Another use of decoupage was the decoration of dummy and chimney boards – life-sized flat wooden figures and shapes decorated to resemble soldiers, children, servants and animals. The earliest ones are thought to date from the 17th century, and although most were painted, decoupage was also a popular method of decoration. Horace Walpole wrote in 1757 of a Mr Muntz who had 'done nothing this summer but paste two chimney boards'.

Eighteenth-century decoupers worked their craft with the intention of imitating more expensive wares, and well-executed decoupage is often mistaken for painting. The technique evolved due to the popularity of hand-painted Chinese lacquerware. It was soon discovered that imitations of the original imported

*Miniature trays by Angela Shaw show
the diversity of decoupage, set against
natural and painted backgrounds with
decorated borders.*

pieces could be made in papier mâché and decorated with decoupage at a fraction of the cost. The entire piece of furniture – usually a desk – would be covered in gesso and then decorated with hand-tinted or painted prints. This new art form was given the pejorative name of Art Provo, or 'poor man's lacquer', yet it was so sought-after that it became more popular than the very furniture it was trying to imitate. Unfortunately, these pieces were often executed in low-quality materials and few examples exist today.

The Georgians decorated their rooms with inexpensive black and white prints which were pasted directly on to cream- or straw-coloured walls. Known as print rooms, the balance and harmony of the prints in them was all-important, and echoed the baroque and classical rococo styles which predominated in the 17th and 18th centuries.

It was Caroline Duer, an editor of Paris *Vogue*, who created an interest in decoupage in America in the early 1900s. She worked in the Biedermeier style, using embossed paper, scrapbook flowers and gold braid paper, and produced some of the finest examples of decoupage existing in the USA today.

In Germany, highly-coloured paper cut-outs were first published in Breslau in the middle of the 19th century. They were known as 'chromos' in France and 'swags' in the United States. These cut-outs were used for decoupage on furniture long before they appeared in Victorian scrap albums.

Decoupage became a very popular hobby in Victorian England, so much so that special scraps were sold, which were used to build up rich compositions on boxes and furniture. Queen Victoria was an avid collector of decoupage, and it became a pastime of the rich and famous. Lord Byron made a decoupage screen with theatrical portraits on one side and prominent boxers of the day on the other; the screen took him three years to complete and was bought a year later in 1815 by his publisher John Murray. There was quite a vogue for such scrap screens during the early 19th century, and sheets of chromolithodie-stamped scraps and decorative borders were published specially for their decoration.

In the early 20th century, artists such as Pablo Picasso and Georges Braque started to use collage to create works of art. Collage comes from the word *coller* – to glue – and is similar to decoupage in its use of cut-outs arranged to create a new composition. However, collage is not restricted to two-dimensional paper cut-outs and may use a variety of dissimilar materials, which are not usually varnished. Collage is now considered a fine art, whereas decoupage is still viewed as an applied art as it is often carried out on boxes or pieces of furniture.

As with many other arts and crafts practised today, people are taking a much broader view of what they want to create and how they want to achieve it. The projects in this book use different methods and mate-

. . . .

This First World War naval hat box decorated by Denise Thomas retains its original colour and the sailor's name on the lid.

rials to produce interesting effects: paint, photocopiers, hand-tinting and collage are all included. Today, we are fortunate in having all the reference materials of the past with all the technology of the present. We are constantly bombarded with visual material suitable for decoupage – posters, magazines, newspapers, wrapping paper, postcards, paper packaging, even carrier bags. Modern varnishes give a better finish than many of the varnishes of the past, and they also dry more quickly. Black and white and colour photocopiers enable designs to be reproduced quickly and fairly inexpensively, and can increase or reduce the size of any image. With all this at your fingertips, you can work in a medium with a long history and yet create a piece that is highly individual and contemporary.

MATERIALS AND EQUIPMENT

THE MATERIALS and equipment needed for decoupage are inexpensive and readily available from arts and crafts stores. It takes very little time to build up a varied selection. The basic items are listed here; more specialized requirements are given in the lists of materials for individual projects.

ITEMS TO DECOUPAGE
You can decoupage almost any surface and any object. It is a craft that can be applied successfully to paper packaging – such as shoe or chocolate boxes; metal – such as old buckets, watering-cans or biscuit (cookie) tins; glass – for instance, vases and bowls; and all kinds of wood objects. It can even be applied to walls, doors, floors and furniture. Look in second-hand stores and sales for old furniture which you can decoupage; alternatively, you could purchase new unpainted containers, such as jewellery boxes, hat boxes and small chests and caskets.

PRINTED MATERIAL
The sources of decorative images for decoupage are almost endless: glossy magazines, old catalogues, postcards, Christmas and birthday cards, books, newspapers and so on are readily available. Old maps and charts, sheet music and botanical drawings also provide interesting motifs, to give just a few examples. Photocopiers can be used to reproduce any image desired, and the results may be used in black and white or hand-tinted with colours. Colour photocopies just need cutting out. Modern copies of old-fashioned 'scraps' may also be purchased from many museum and craft shops.

PRINT SEALERS
Depending on the quality of the paper print used, it may bleed or discolour if not sealed before application. A sealer will turn porous paper into a non-porous surface, making it easier to handle and preventing it from discoloration or yellowing.

SHELLAC: the best sealer is white or blond shellac. Shellac is made from a secretion of the lac insert mixed with methylated spirits, and is a quick-drying sealant.

PRINT FIXATIVES: these can be bought in spray form from good office and stationery suppliers. They come in a matt/flat or gloss finish, and give an acrylic rubber-based coating. They provide a protective coat, minimizing the chances of the print turning yellow with age, and are abrasive-resistant.

ACRYLIC GESSO

You can buy this ready-prepared from artists' suppliers, and it is an alternative (if more expensive) primer to PVA glue or white matt/flat emulsion paint. It gives a thick, smooth chalky layer on which to work, and may be painted or tinted before decouping.

PAINTS

The base material of the object to be decoupaged will, to some degree, dictate the paint to be used, but there are various options available depending on the effect required. Most projects in this book specify water-based emulsions and acrylics. Although oil-based paints tend to render a more brilliant colour, water-based paints are easier to work with, as they can be thinned with water. Oil-based paints require a solvent such as white spirit for thinning and cleaning brushes.

PRIMER AND UNDERCOAT: special metal and wood primers can be purchased from decorators' suppliers. White undercoat is used on unvarnished wood that has first been primed. With all paints, allow each coat to dry thoroughly before applying successive coats, to ensure an even result.

EMULSION, MATT/FLAT WOOD, AND GLOSS PAINTS: emulsion is used for the majority of the projects in this book as a base for decoupage, in matt/flat or silk finish. When using gloss on wood, it is best to use a primer and an undercoat as well. Matt/flat wood paint can be used instead of gloss on wood surfaces.

ACRYLIC PAINTS are quick-drying and come in many colours. They may be used to add extra decoration to decoupaged surfaces. They can be mixed with water, but an acrylic medium will keep the colours stronger.

ARTISTS' OIL PAINTS are slow to dry and quite expensive, so are best used on small areas to add tints with crackle glaze. Some oil-based paints also contain lead, and so should not be used on items that will be used by children.

ENAMEL PAINTS are good for metal objects, as are specialist ceramic and glass paints. Metal should be treated all over with a metal primer before adding the base colour.

CAR SPRAY PAINTS are a good way of applying colour quickly and evenly, but must be used in a well-ventilated room.

VARNISHES

A polyurethane clear wood varnish will give a durable finish to decoupage work. It is available in matt/flat, satin or gloss finishes: matt/flat will give a soft, flat effect; satin, soft but with a slight sheen; and gloss a high shine to the finish. Varnish is available yellow, clear or even tinted. It may be purchased from decorators' suppliers; a non-toxic version is recommended.

ARTISTS' ACRYLIC VARNISH: also known as picture varnish, and comes in matt/flat or gloss. It is more expensive than ordinary varnish but does not yellow with age.

PVA GLUE may be diluted and used as a varnish, particularly for projects on glass and wallpaper.

COLOURED VARNISH: oak and antique pine varnishes can be used to age decoupaged objects; rub off after painting on to leave a residue of varnish behind.

CRACKLE VARNISH is an effect produced by two varnishes, usually sold as a pack, which work against one another to create a decorative crackle finish. Artists' oils may be used to fill in the cracks with colour; burnt umber or sienna are particularly effective.

WAX is also available for final polishing, both as standard beeswax and in a variety of other finishes. Wax should be applied to paint which is completely dry, using a soft cloth and small circular movements. The first coat should be quite thick and left to dry for a few hours before rubbing off; repeat two or three times, with a thinner layer and less drying time.

CLEANING MATERIALS

METHYLATED SPIRIT is used to dilute shellac and is also used for washing brushes, depending on the type of paint used.

WHITE SPIRIT OR TURPENTINE is a clear solvent used to dilute oil-based paints and for washing brushes and cleaning objects to be decoupaged.

GLUES

PVA OR WHITE GLUE dries rapidly, and may be used at full strength or diluted with water, two parts water to one part PVA. Also known as polyvinyl acetate woodworking glue.

WALLPAPER PASTE is not as strong as PVA glue, but it sometimes contains a fungicide which prevents mould, although this also makes it unsuitable for children.

SPRAY ADHESIVE is very clean and fast to use, but should be carefully directed and used in a well-ventilated room.

BRUSHES

Large and medium-sized household or decorators' brushes are used for applying colour and varnish to larger surfaces. Buy the best-quality brush you can or the work may be spoilt by loose hairs caught in the varnish. Keep brushes for different jobs separate from one another and label them so that you know you have one brush for sealer, one for paint, and another for varnish. Fine artists' brushes are needed for hand-tinting prints. Clean brushes in water (if water-based) or white spirit (if oil-based) immediately after use.

OTHER EQUIPMENT

CRAFT KNIFE OR SCALPEL: these fine-bladed sharp knives, also known as utility knives with snap-off blades, may be used with care for cutting a straight border or line, or for cutting out intricate detail. Blades should be protected when stored.

SANDPAPER is needed for rubbing down surfaces before decoupage and for sanding down between layers of paint and varnish. It is available in various grades from fine to coarse.

RUBBER ROLLER/LINO ROLLER OR ROLLING PIN is useful for pushing the glued print into position, and ensuring that it is stuck down flat and firmly.

PHOTOCOPIER: although not strictly necessary, access to a photocopier is strongly recommended if you need several copies of the same motif or if you do not wish to stick original images on to an object.

SCISSORS

(b) small

(a) large

TWEEZERS

LINING PAPER

PVA GLUE

ACRYLIC PAINTS

PRINT FIX

GREEN EMULSION PAINT

DUTCH GOLD

PENCIL

POLYURETHANE VARNISH

CRAFT KNIVES

GOLD SIZE

RULER

CRACKLE VARNISH

APPLICATOR

STRONG GLUE

WOOD FILLER

ANTIQUE VARNISH

GOLD SPRAY PAINT

CLEAR VARNISH

BLACKBOARD PAINT

ANTIQUE GOLD METALLIC PAINT

SPRAY ADHESIVE

SPONGE

COLOUR CARDS

WHITE GLOSS PAINT

BRUSHES

MASKING TAPE

BASIC TECHNIQUES

BEFORE YOU start on a project, make sure you have everything to hand. It is a good idea to protect the work surface with a large sheet of polythene, to prevent it from getting sticky. Try to work in a well-ventilated room, especially when using varnish, spray paints and spray adhesive.

DESIGN AND COMPOSITION

Decoupage is a craft requiring little or no drawing ability to produce spectacular results. The joy of this craft is that with a little planning and an eye for composition, an ugly or boring object can be trans-formed into something beautiful.

It is a good idea to draw the object to be decorated on to paper and then to cut and arrange the pieces to be decoupaged on to this. When you have a pleasing composition, you can then draw round the shapes and use them as a guide when working on the actual piece. Alternatively, secure the pieces into place on the object using blu-tack/low-tack peel. When the right com-position has been obtained, you can remove the blu-tack/low-tack peel and stick each piece exactly into position.

SEALING PAPER PRINTS

Before cutting, the print should be sealed to prevent discoloration. It will also strengthen the print so that it will not disintegrate when handled or covered in glue or paste. Strengthening the paper will also make the cutting of delicate pieces much easier. Either use a spray print fixative or paint on a coat of shellac.

THINNING THICK PRINTS

Prints should be as thin as possible for decoupage. If you wish to use a postcard or an image on a thick piece of paper or card, use the following reduction method.

*First, seal the print on the front side
(as described above).*

. . . .

*Next, coat the wrong side with PVA
or white glue, and leave to dry.*

. . . .

On the wrong side of the print, lift up a corner of the card using a craft knife or fingernail. Place a pencil across it and, starting from one corner, roll the card around the pencil until it is tight. Keep rolling until a layer of paper has been removed.

. . . .

PREPARING SURFACES

Before decoupage can be applied, items may need to be prepared in various ways.

VARNISHED OR WAXED ITEMS: wash the surface with white spirit to avoid any adhesion problems. If the furniture is blistered or split, it may then need filling with a wood filler. Sand when dry and seal with shellac. Wash the surface once more with white spirit when dry.

PAINTED WOOD: previously well-treated wood will need very little treatment other than wiping the surface with white spirit. If it has bumps and blemishes, it may also need to be rubbed down with a very fine sandpaper. If the paintwork is bad, it will need sanding and then repainting.

NEW METAL: rinse the object in a solution of one part water to one part vinegar. Dry thoroughly and then brush on two coats of rust-resistant paint. When the paint is dry, sand with a fine-grade sandpaper. Wipe with a soft cloth.

OLD METAL: use heavy-duty steel wool to clean off the rust spots, then treat as for new metal.

CERAMIC: no special preparations are necessary, but make sure that the surface is free of dust and grease.

PRIMING

To create a clean, even surface for decoupage a layer of paint is usually applied. Apply white matt/flat emulsion paint or ready-prepared acrylic gesso to prime a porous surface and to provide a surface for the decoupage. Use a decorators' brush for emulsion paint and a soft artists' brush for gesso. Allow to dry thoroughly between layers.

CUTTING

Always cut out the print with a large surround, using large scissors. Change to fine scissors for detailed cutting. A craft knife or scalpel can also be used for intricate pieces of decoupage work.

STICKING

Apply a layer of glue to the back of the print. Use tweezers to pick up and position very small or delicate pieces of print; scissors can be used for less fragile pieces. Once the paper is applied, cover with a soft cloth and run a roller over the prints to get rid of any air bubbles. Check that all the cut-outs are stuck down well. If they are not, put a tiny amount of glue on the end of a cocktail stick or toothpick, slip it under the print, and roll under.

VARNISHING AND POLISHING

Decoupage may be varnished with anything from two to twenty coats of varnish. The quality of varnish generally available in most decorators' shops is so good that only a few coats are usually necessary. The varnish must be allowed to dry in a dust-free atmosphere between coats. About ten coats may be applied. Sanding is required. Sand with the grain, clean with a damp cloth and then varnish again. Wax may also be used as a final polish.

Paint must be absolutely dry before you apply the varnish. Use a standard household paint brush and apply with smooth, even strokes in one direction, and avoid letting the varnish drip or accumulate around edges. Apply an even coat over the whole piece, working in two stages if necessary so that you can stand the piece on a dry edge or surface when drying.

GALLERY

The following pages illustrate the variety of work produced by contemporary decoupage artists. Some of the pieces were made by traditional methods, working on existing objects and with the finished design given many coats of varnish and polished to a mirror-like surface. Other artists have created the actual objects they decoupage and use fewer coats of varnish. The visual imagery employed ranges from traditional and classical motifs to the shocking, surreal and even kitsch.

The following designs will provide you with an idea of the versatility of decoupage, and as the basic techniques are so simple, inspire you to experiment and develop your own ideas.

~

Folding Screen
NICOLA WINGATE SAUL
Screens provide a perfect background for decoupage. This artist uses original prints for her screens; the botanical drawings used here are complemented by the colour scheme, chosen to give a classical feel in keeping with the object.

Print Column

NICOLA WINGATE SAUL

The pale straw colour of the base is that traditionally used in Georgian print rooms. The bands of print-room patterns decorating the column continue in the form of borders on the base and the top, creating a contemporary piece with a traditional feel.

. . . .

Large Urn

JULIETTE PIERCE

Juliette makes her own bowls and pots from layers of papier mâché built up around frames of card or chicken wire. The decoupage takes place after the final coat of base colour has been applied. This artist often personalizes her decoupage prints by drawing on them before sticking them into place.

. . . .

Ribbon Heart Box

JOSEPHINE WHITFIELD

This wooden box was painted before being decoupaged with a large flower print. Josephine then painted a ribbon surrounding the lid and flowing down the sides of the box. A similar design could be worked with real ribbon stuck into position with a strong glue.

· · · ·

Rabbits

GLOBAL VILLAGE

Comics provide the decoration on these papier mâché rabbits. Decoupage work such as this is carried out in an Indonesian rural community for export to the West. Although all the shapes are the same, the finishes of individual pieces vary.

· · · ·

Marine Box

NICOLA WINGATE SAUL
Colour, motif and composition are well balanced in this decoupaged piece. The cream-coloured box is decoupaged with a decoration of print-room borders and central motifs are of fish and other sea creatures. The design continues inside the box.

. . . .

Room Fan

JULIET HELEN WALKER
This exquisite fan is 1.2m (4ft) wide. It is made from a variety of papers, which are then applied with decoupage, producing an elaborate and beautiful room decoration.

. . . .

Clothes Box, Tray and Magazine Rack

ROB TURNER, CELESTIAL STUDIO

These three pieces are characteristic of the artist's work, with mono-chromatic prints and themes of stars and cherubs decoupaged on to a black background.

. . . .

Candlestick and Mirror

MIKE CHANDLER

These pieces are decorated with decoupage and paint. The black and white prints and use of vibrant red, yellow and blue paints are an unusual but successful combination and make an interesting composition.

. . . .

Decoupage Pieces

STEVE WRIGHT

Steve Wright is internationally known for his work, and his designs are photographed and turned into wrapping paper and cards. He works on most surfaces, including walls, furniture and paper. The imagery shown here is typical of his work – a combination of pop culture and royal and religious iconography.

. . . .

Small Oval Boxes

EMMA WHITFIELD

Almost jewel-like in appearance, these plywood boxes have been painted royal blue and decorated with Elizabethan miniatures, photocopied from a book on the subject.

. . . .

Cupid Boxes

EMMA WHITFIELD

These beautiful boxes have been painted cream and then given a coat of crackle varnish. The cracks are then rubbed with a burnt umber oil paint to give definition. Finally, the cut-out Valentine images of hearts and cupids are applied.

. . . .

Solicitor's Deed Box

DENISE THOMAS

An excellent example of traditional decoupage, this piece is painted, aged with crackle varnish and then decorated with flowers and fruits.

. . . .

1954 Army Mess Tin

DENISE THOMAS

Painted a cream colour, aged with crackle varnish and then decoupaged with fruits and flowers followed by many coats of varnish, a once-mundane object is transformed into one of real beauty.

. . . .

Blue Table and Clock

JOSEPHINE WHITFIELD

This small table was painted a powder blue and decorated using teacup motifs. The clock complements the shape of the prints, extending and emphasizing the imagery.

. . . .

Three-legged Table

ANGELA SHAW

Painted in Wedgwood
green, and treated with
crackle varnish, the top of
this table is decoupaged
with an intricate design of
flowers. The inside edges
and the moulding of the
support are painted gold.

. . . .

Flower Board

KATHY WEBSTER
AND ROSY BURMAN

This floral dummy board is
given a three-dimensional
appearance through the
combination of images
taken from wallpaper
designs. The board is then
oil-glazed and varnished.

. . . .

VICTORIAN TRAY

EMMA WHITFIELD

THE RICH green background and full-blown flowers of this tray are typical of traditional decoupage. The background flowers are cut out of wrapping paper in one piece and then varnished, with additional flowers cut out individually and added in layers. By building up different layers of varnish and flowers, the finished pattern appears to be in relief and any gaps in the design are easily filled.

~

MATERIALS AND EQUIPMENT

● *wooden tray* ● *fine sand-paper* ● *cloth* ● *white wood primer* ● *white undercoat* ● *green matt/flat emulsion paint* ● *brushes for painting, gluing and varnishing* ● *flowery wrapping paper, and images from magazines and gardening catalogues* ● *scissors* ● *print fixative* ● *spray adhesive* ● *poly-urethane varnish*

. . . . . .

1 The tray chosen does not have to be brand-new and unpainted: an unattractive pattern or colour can be completely covered by the new design.

2 Rub the tray with fine sandpaper and then wipe with a cloth before giving it a coat of primer. Leave the paint to dry. Repeat the process, including sanding, using an undercoat.

3 When the undercoat is dry and has been rubbed down, paint on a coat of green emulsion. Leave this to dry. A second coat may be applied for a deeper colour.

4 Cut out large background flowers from one piece of wrapping paper and seal the images with a print fixative.

5 Check that the cut-outs fit on to the tray and adjust if necessary. Spray the back of each cut-out with a spray adhesive – this is a quick and clean way of applying glue to such a large piece of paper.

6 Stick the cut-outs to the base of the tray. When they are in position, push down firmly on to the tray. Work from one end to the other to avoid bubbles or wrinkles in the middle.

7 Cut out smaller flowers from other pieces of wrapping paper. Use any remaining scraps from the first piece as well, or look through other sources such as magazines and catalogues. Seal with a print fixative.

8 Varnish over the base layer of flowers, then leave to dry before going on to the next stage.

9 Apply spray adhesive to the back of the smaller flowers and stick into position. Varnish once more and leave to dry again.

10 Continue building up the composition with different images, varnishing after each additional layer. Here, butterflies were added for variety.

11 Apply and varnish the final images. When the desired composition has been achieved, brush again with varnish. When dry, sand the whole tray with a very fine sandpaper. Brush away any dust and then varnish again. Repeat this six or seven times until the tray is as smooth as a mirror.

HEART BOXES

EMMA WHITFIELD

THIS PRETTY set of nesting heart-shaped trinket boxes has been decorated with facsimile Victorian scraps. The scraps were reduced on a photocopier, because the originals were too large for these small boxes. The plywood bases have been completely transformed by a coat of varnish, giving the boxes the richness of pine and a more substantial appearance.

It is not essential to use heart-shaped boxes – similar nesting boxes can be purchased in oval, round or square shapes. They make beautiful gifts in themselves or they can be used as presentation boxes for jewellery.

~

MATERIALS AND EQUIPMENT

• *heart-shaped plywood boxes* • *fine sandpaper* • *PVA glue* • *brushes for gluing and varnishing* • *Victorian-style scraps and images* • *scissors* • *craft knife* • *print fixative* • *yellow-tinted polyurethane varnish*

. . . . . .

1 The plywood boxes may differ slightly in colour but by the time the images are stuck on and a coat of varnish is added, the tone will appear the same on all of them. Remove any rough edges with fine sandpaper.

2 Brush off any dust from the surface of the boxes. Seal the lids and sides with a coat of PVA glue. Leave the glue to dry, and then seal the insides and bases. Leave to dry once more.

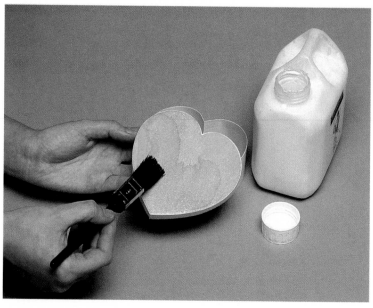

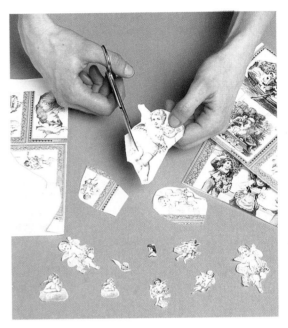

3 For small-scale projects such as this, delicate and intricate images look best. It may be necessary to use a colour photo-copier and reduce the size of some of the images to fit the smaller boxes.

4 Once there are enough images in the correct sizes, cut them out. In places where it is difficult to manipulate scissors use a craft knife instead. Seal the images with print fixative.

5 Using PVA glue, stick the images on to the lids and around the sides of the bases. If you want the boxes to have the same design, work on the largest one first and use it as a guide for the others.

6 When the images are dry, the box can be given a coat of varnish. For more depth of colour, leave the varnish to dry between coats. Sand with fine sandpaper and varnish again.

HAT BOX

EMMA WHITFIELD

Hat boxes are not just for hats: they can be used to store all kinds of things, from wool or needlework supplies, to gloves or even socks. The box here is made from thin cardboard and was obtained from a mail order company, but many large department stores also sell a range of hat boxes at very reasonable prices. These can be easily customized with decoupage. Here, hand-tinted photocopies create a piece reminiscent of an illuminated manuscript or a richly coloured piece of stained glass, with strong jewel-like colours set against a black background.

~

MATERIALS AND EQUIPMENT

● *hat box* ● *black emulsion paint* ● *brushes for painting and gluing* ● *ruler* ● *tape measure* ● *black and white photocopies* ● *scissors* ● *print fixative* ● *PVA glue* ● *acrylic paints*

. . . . . .

1 Large cardboard hat boxes are obtainable by mail-order or from most department stores. Any plain cardboard box could be given similar treatment, so collect old boxes from shops and supermarkets and decorate these.

2 Paint the lid of the box – a gloss was used here, but you can also use matt/flat or silk, depending on the desired finish. Do not paint the side of the lid, as the decoupage design continues on to it.

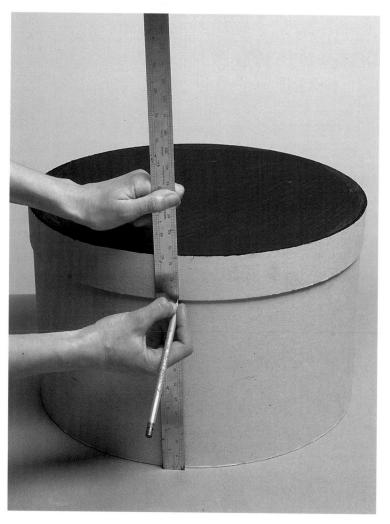

3 Measure the depth of the box up to the lid, and the depth of the lid. You can then cut the design to fit the box exactly. Measure the perimeter of the box with a tape measure to work out the number of photocopies needed to cover it.

4 Photocopy the pictures for the box. Measure the picture and cut it so that a narrow strip will fit the side of the lid, and the rest around the sides of the box. Seal the images with a print fixative, then glue the narrow strip around the side of the lid.

5 Glue the larger sections of the photocopied images around the side of the box, until completely covered. Make sure that the paper is stuck flat all the way around. This is quite difficult to achieve when using large sheets of paper.

6 Use acrylic paints diluted with water to tint the white areas of the photocopy. If preferred, gold or silver paint could be used. When the paints are dry the box may be given a protective coat of diluted PVA glue.

Dressing room Screen

EMMA WHITFIELD

An old-fashioned folding screen can be stylish, functional and versatile. It need not be reserved for a dressing room: a screen may be used as a room divider in a studio apartment to create the illusion of a little extra space, or it can hide an unsightly corner. This old screen was originally found in a second-hand sale, covered with stained and tattered green canvas. The canvas was removed and the screen was filled, sanded, primed and topcoated before having decoupage applied. The deep red of the screen complements the gold borders and classical prints for an antique feel.

~

MATERIALS AND EQUIPMENT

- *screen* ● *white wood primer*
- *white wood undercoat*
- *maroon matt/flat emulsion paint* ● *brushes for painting, gluing and varnishing*
- *classical prints* ● *scissors*
- *pencil* ● *ruler* ● *PVA glue*
- *gold paper* ● *craft knife (optional)* ● *print fixative*
- *antique varnish* ● *sponge*
- *clear glue* ● *ribbon*

. . . . . .

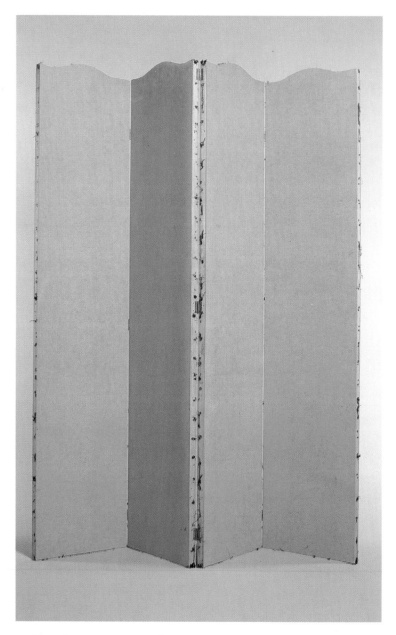

1 If you buy a screen second-hand, remove any fabric if it is stained or old. Remove as many of the old tacks as possible, using the back of a claw hammer. If the tacks cannot be removed, hammer them in as far as possible and cover with a ribbon at a later stage.

2 Prime each panel of the front and back of the screen in turn, and leave to dry. When dry, apply an undercoat and leave to dry again.

3 Starting from the top of the screen and using even strokes, paint on the topcoat. A rich maroon is used here. Different colours and designs could be used for the front and the back of the screen.

4 Cut out the images to be used as decoupage. Here, copies of classical Greek and Roman figures and architectural details are used. Specialist decoupage books have images such as these which can be cut out and used directly or photocopied and enlarged for bigger projects.

5 Using a pencil and ruler, draw faint lines across the screen to mark the intended position of each picture. These can be erased later. Using PVA glue, stick each picture in place.

6 Place the ruler its own width away from the edge of the gold paper. Put pressure on the ruler and tear strips of paper against the edge to create the border strips for the screen. For a crisper-looking edge, use a ruler and craft knife.

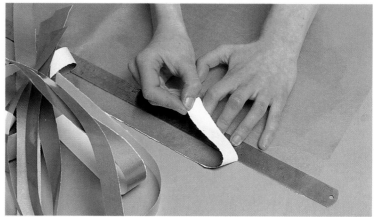

7 Stick the gold border around the edges of the frame. Where the top edge of the screen curves, you may need to mitre the corners – in other words, cut out V-shaped sections, like making darts in dressmaking.

8 Seal the prints with a print fixative to help protect them and stop them lifting when the antiquing takes place.

9 Using a brush, apply antique varnish to the whole of the screen. Do not leave it to dry.

10 Dab the surface of the screen with a sponge to give the antique varnish a mottled effect.

11 Measure around all the edges of the screen to calculate the amount of ribbon needed. Using a clear glue, stick on the ribbon to cover up any old nails and holes.

KITCHEN CHAIR

JOSEPHINE WHITFIELD

BY CLEVER use of decoupage, with a stained varnish to give an aged appearance, an old kitchen chair can be transformed into a very desirable object. The images for this project have been chosen for a country feel: fruits and butterflies. The fruit lies in a cluster along the back and around the seat of the chair, while the butterflies are placed at random to look as though they have just settled. Look for similar pictures in seed catalogues, old gardening books and magazines, or even on wrapping paper. Colour photocopies of Old Master prints are particularly effective.

~

MATERIALS AND EQUIPMENT

● *an old chair* ● *white primer*
● *white undercoat* ● *cream
matt/flat emulsion paint*
● *colour images* ● *scissors*
● *craft knife* ● *print fixative*
● *PVA glue* ● *yellow-tinted
varnish* ● *brushes for painting,
gluing and varnishing* ● *cloth*

. . . . . .

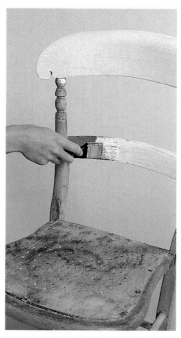

1 An old battered wooden chair can be transformed with decoupage. If necessary, fill and sand the chair before commencing decoration; alternatively, a new kitchen chair may be treated in the same way as the one in the project.

2 Remove any dust with a damp cloth, then paint the chair with a protective coat of primer. Leave this to dry before applying an undercoat. Once the undercoat is dry, the top coat may be applied.

3 Cut out the pictures. The larger shapes can be cut with scissors, but for the more intricate shapes such as antennae on butterflies, a craft knife may be easier to use. Seal the images with a print fixative.

4 Arrange and rearrange the pictures on a flat surface until the composition looks good. Take each component and, using PVA glue, stick on to the chair back.

5 Stick the remaining pictures around the seat, legs and uprights of the chair. Make sure the images are stuck down well and that there are no bumps and folds in the paper. As chairs come in for a great deal of wear and tear, it is important that each stage of the work is done properly.

6 When the glue is dry, paint on the tinted varnish. There are a variety of tinted or stained varnishes on the market – some of them are even coloured red or green. The one used here is a warm-toned yellow varnish.

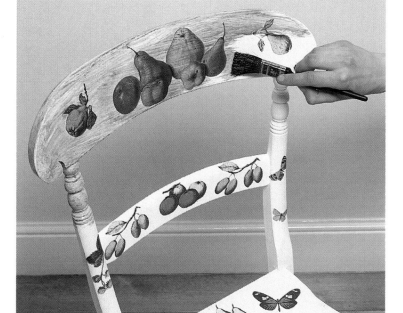

7 While the varnish is still wet, rub it with a cloth. This will remove the excess varnish and allow highlights on the design.

FLORAL MIRROR

JOSEPHINE WHITFIELD

THIS STRIKING mirror was once part of an old wardrobe. The flaking paint and the scratches on the mirror demanded an ingenious design to cover up the faults and create an attractive piece in its own right. The resulting mirror – although more collage than decoupage in the purest sense – is a perfect example of a contemporary version of a traditional decorative craft. Old skills are combined with modern materials to create a new mirror. The design is based on stylized tulips and leaves which entwine around the mirror frame down on to the mirror itself. The brightly-coloured card shapes were put on a black background and then toned down with a wash of black oil paint, linseed oil and white spirit.

~

MATERIALS AND EQUIPMENT

● *old mirror* ● *wood filler*
● *brushes for filling,*
painting, gluing and
varnishing ● *sandpaper*
● *wood primer* ● *dark under-*
coat ● *masking tape* ● *matt*
black emulsion paint ● *tracing*
paper ● *pencil* ● *white paper*
● *scissors* ● *thin card in*
various colours ● *blu-tack/*
low-tack peel ● *PVA glue*
● *polyurethane varnish*
● *black oil paint* ● *white*
spirit ● *linseed oil* ● *sponge*
. . . . . .

1 For this project, an old mirror
is as good as a new one, because
if the mirror itself is not perfect,
any blemishes can be covered by
clever use of decoupage.

2 Fill any holes, such as
indentations left from old
hinges or locks, with wood filler.
Leave this to harden.

3 Remove any flaky paint. When
the wood filler is hard, sand the
surface around the mirror along
with the filler. The easiest way to
sand is by wrapping the sandpaper
around a block of wood.

4 Paint a coat of primer on the
bare patches of wood. Leave to
dry, then paint on undercoat over
all the wood.

5 Apply masking tape all around the edge of the mirror, to prevent the glass being covered in paint. Paint on the topcoat. Emulsion paint was used here for a matt/flat finish, but eggshell or gloss may be used.

6 Draw or trace the required designs on to white paper, and cut them out as templates. Use as a guide to cutting the shapes from coloured card.

7 To save time, the card may be folded before cutting out the flowers and leaves, so several images can be cut out at once.

8 Use blu-tack/low-tack peel to
arrange the flowers and foliage
into a pleasing composition on the
mirror frame.

9 Arrange the flowers and leaves
to fall on to the mirror,
covering up any flaws or scratches.

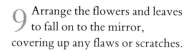

10 Using PVA glue, stick each
flower and leaf into
position. Remove the blu-tack/
low-tack peel as you work.

11 When all the glue is dry, give the mirror frame a coat of varnish. Use a fine brush to varnish the pieces stuck on to the mirror, to avoid splashing varnish on to the glass itself.

12 For a more subtle, aged effect, mix black oil paint with a little white spirit and linseed oil. Gently dab this on to the mirror frame with a sponge when the varnish has dried.

CELESTIAL CLOCK

JOSEPHINE WHITFIELD

THIS WONDERFUL clock is made from a scrap piece of MDF (medium-density fibreboard), a clock mechanism and part of a book jacket. The clock hands are decorated with a paper sun and moon in keeping with the astrological theme on the clock face, and the surrounding edges have been coated with Dutch gold. The result is a highly desirable object made at very little expense.

Choose a design to reflect the style of the clock's surroundings: flowers for a conservatory, toys for a child's room, or even wallpaper to match a room in the house. The clock can be bought in kit form and runs on a battery.

~

MATERIALS AND EQUIPMENT

- *piece of MDF* • *D-clamp*
- *saw* • *ruler* • *pencil* • *drill*
- *astrological chart or other large image* • *fine and coarse sandpaper* • *scissors* • *print fixative* • *gold size* • *Dutch gold* • *craft knife* • *PVA glue* • *brush for gluing*
- *piece of stiff black paper*
- *clock mechanism with hands*

. . . . . .

1 Measure the size of the image for the clock face and use this measurement to determine the size of the clock. Draw the measurement on the MDF, and then secure it to a work surface using a D-clamp. Cut out the MDF with a saw.

2 With a ruler and pencil, draw a line across the diagonal from one corner to the other. Repeat from the other corner. Where the two lines cross, drill a hole large enough for the 'hand' part of the clock mechanism to pass through. Sand the edges of the hole and around the MDF piece.

3 Cut out the image which will be used to make the clock face. If you do not wish to destroy the original image, it can be photocopied. Seal the image with a print fixative.

4 Using the cut-out picture as a guide, draw around it in pencil on the MDF. Remove the picture. The corners around the circle will be painted gold.

5 Apply gold size to the corners surrounding the circle. Leave for between 15 and 20 minutes until it begins to get tacky. Lay the Dutch gold on to the size and press down firmly with your thumb. Remove the backing paper and trim the edges with a craft knife.

6 Spread glue on to the back of the picture and stick it in place. Feel for the hole in the centre of the clock and, using a sharp pencil, make a hole by pushing from the front of the clock to the back.

7 Draw the motifs for the hands in black paper. Cut them out and glue into place, one on the end of the minute hand and one on the end of the hour hand. Assemble the clock mechanism according to the instructions; do not forget to put a battery in it!

DECOUPAGE TIN

MARION ELLIOT

IT IS HARD to believe that this appealing tin was once just an ordinary biscuit (cookie) tin. It has been completely transformed by the imaginative use of brightly coloured Indian packaging, cut out and arranged to form a pleasing composition. Although this tin is still used for its original purpose, it could store other items such as bills and letters, dried herbs or sewing equipment.

Unusual packaging from other countries can be used in this way to decorate all kinds of tins and boxes. Collect paper ephemera when abroad and use it for decoupage when you return home.

~

MATERIALS AND EQUIPMENT

- *biscuit (cookie) tin* • *white metal primer or car spray paint* • *brushes for painting, gluing and varnishing*
- *brightly coloured packaging*
- *scissors* • *print fixative*
- *PVA glue* • *polyurethane varnish (optional)*

• • • • • •

1 Use any biscuit or cookie tin for this project; it does not matter if it is already decorated as the new design will cover it. Make sure the tin is clean inside and out and that any labels have been removed.

2 Paint the lid and the outside of the tin base with a coat of white metal primer. As an alternative, car spray paint may be used, but this must be applied in a well-ventilated area. Leave to dry. If the paint appears streaked, add a second coat.

3 The decoration for the tin may be chosen according to a colour scheme – warm reds, yellows, and oranges, for example – or to a particular theme, as here. This packaging comes from a variety of Indian products – food, incense sticks and hair oil.

4 Carefully cut out the individual elements which will make up the final composition. If repeat motifs are needed, these may be photocopied in colour. Seal the images with a print fixative.

5 Arrange the separate elements to form a composition over the painted surfaces of the tin. The design does not have to be symmetrical: here the top of the tin is a free arrangement while the sides of the tin form a pattern.

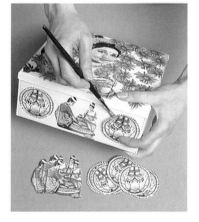

6 Glue into place each individual piece of paper and check the edges to make sure they are not lifting anywhere. If they are not stuck properly, push a brush with a spot of glue under the edge of the paper, remove the brush and then apply more pressure to the area.

7 When the glue is dry, paint on a coat of varnish or PVA glue diluted with one-third water.

Circus Frieze

MARION ELLIOT

This frieze is designed for a child's room. It is made up of unusually rich colours, with a bright green background and a red and gold border as a change from more traditional pastel colours usually associated with nursery rooms. The frieze is deeper than most shop-bought ones, as it is cut out of a width of lining paper. A book of traditional borders supplied the designs for the edges, which were enlarged and photocopied in colour, while images from an old-fashioned circus – clowns, tigers and dancing ponies – decorate the centre. The joy of making a frieze like this is that all the images can be cut out and stuck into place on the flat, and then glued as a completed frieze into position on the wall.

~

MATERIALS AND EQUIPMENT

● *lining paper* ● *ruler*
● *pencil* ● *green emulsion
paint* ● *brushes for painting
and gluing* ● *pictures for the
central theme* ● *print fixative*
● *borders, photocopied in
colour or hand-tinted*
● *scissors* ● *PVA glue*

. . . . . .

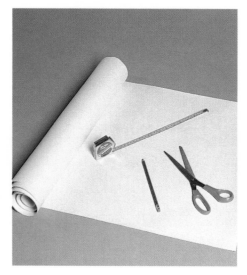

1 You will need lining paper as the basis of the frieze. The paper is used across its width, so find out the length of each roll to calculate how many you will need for a complete room.

2 Mark out the position on the paper for the two borders and the central motifs. This is particularly important if you are going to have a repeating pattern along the frieze.

3 Paint the background with emulsion paint. The pencil marks should be only just visible.

4 Cut out the images for the
centre of the frieze. If you do
not wish to use a circus theme,
choose an alphabet, pictures of toys
or any other appealing motifs. Seal
with a print fixative.

5 Cut out the borders, seal with a
print fixative and stick them
along either edge of the paper.

6 Stick down the central motifs
using the faint pencil marks as a
positioning guide.

7 Seal the whole frieze, including
the painted area, with a coat of
diluted PVA glue.

JEWELLERY BOX

MARION ELLIOT

SMALL CASKETS are covetable items and are even more desirable when decorated with rich patterns. Here, several copies of the same image are used to cover all the surfaces. The sea and fish theme continues inside the box, making it as appealing open as closed. Small wooden boxes such as these are available by mail order or from some department stores, and make ideal gifts for adults and children alike.

~

MATERIALS AND EQUIPMENT

- *wooden box* - *white wood primer* - *white undercoat*
- *white matt/flat wood paint*
- *brushes for painting, gluing and varnishing* - *fine sandpaper* - *marine images*
- *print fixative* - *scissors*
- *PVA glue* - *polyurethane varnish*

. . . . . .

1 A small unvarnished box is needed for this project. The one used here has a curved, hinged lid, but others can be bought with flat lids, and in different shapes and sizes. The lock and brass fittings are appealing features but are not essential to the design.

2 Give the box a coat of primer, and leave to dry before painting on the under- and topcoats, allowing time to dry between each stage. Sand with fine sandpaper to a smooth surface, and repeat all stages on the inside of the box. Seal the images with print fixative.

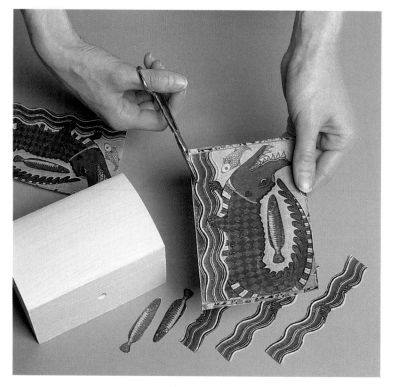

3 Decorate the lid of the box: trim the chosen image to fit, and stick into place with PVA glue.

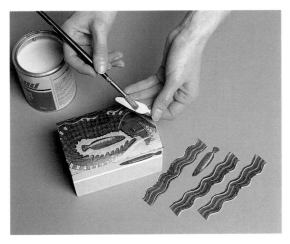

4 Continue decorating the sides of the lid by gluing the cut-out images into place. Here, details of fish are used.

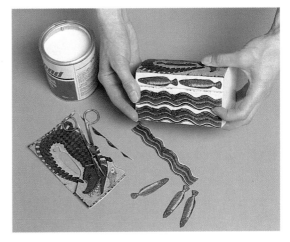

5 Now work on the four sides of the box. This design used sections of the sea, joined together to form a continuous wave.

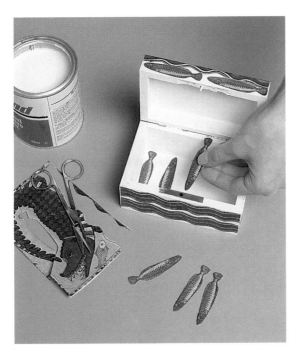

6 Complete the design by decorating the inside of the box in the same way.

7 Apply varnish to the outside of the box, and leave to dry with the lid open to prevent it sticking. Then varnish the inside of the box, and allow to dry before varnishing the base.

WASTE-PAPER BASKET

JOSEPHINE WHITFIELD

WITTY USE of decoupage transforms an ordinary waste-paper bin or basket into a strikingly original object. The imagery is taken from anywhere and everywhere – books, magazines, sweet and candy wrappers, and textured paper. Photocopies are mixed with magazine cut-outs without any regard for scale and proportion. The result is humorous and surrealistic, and will be sure to brighten the dullest days at the office or in the study.

~

MATERIALS AND EQUIPMENT

- *plain waste-paper bin (basket)* ● *lining paper*
- *masking tape* ● *craft knife*
- *scissors* ● *cut-outs from magazines, wrapping paper, holiday ephemera etc* ● *print fixative* ● *blu-tack/low-tack peel* ● *PVA glue* ● *brush for gluing and varnishing*
- *polyurethane varnish*
- *strong glue* ● *cord with tassel trim*

. . . . . .

1 A plain metal waste-paper bin (basket) is used for this project. Any similar one may be used, but it must not be woven or made of basket-work.

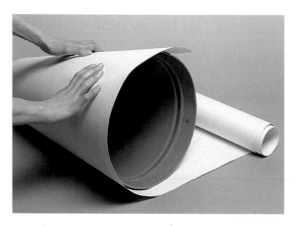

2 The decoupage is worked on a piece of lining paper, which is then stuck on to the bin (waste-paper basket). This enables the composition to be viewed as a whole (and also means the design can be photocopied and repeated on other bins if desired). Measure the paper to fit around the bin.

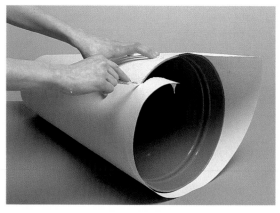

3 Hold the two edges in place with masking tape and trim away the excess paper using a craft knife.

4 Cut out the images – figures, buildings, mountains, cars, surreal 'features' and so on. It is a good idea to have some kind of idea what the composition is to be about before starting on the project. Seal the images with a print fixative.

5 Position the background on to the lining paper using blu-tack/ low-tack peel, starting with the sky, houses and then the street.

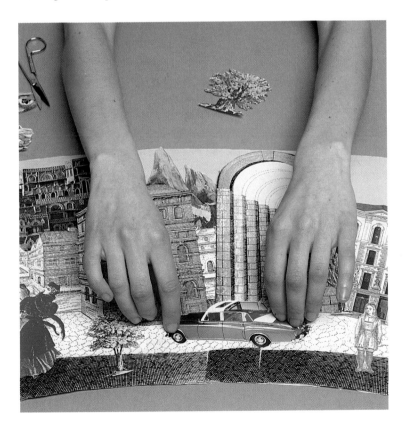

6 Next, add the foreground. This includes cars, figures, trees and pavements. None of the pieces is stuck down at this stage as you will want to rearrange and juggle the pieces to fit them together in the best arrangement.

7 Begin to add the elements which make the composition surreal: perhaps flying fish, large feet and women in swimsuits diving into buildings. When the composition is as you want it, glue down each element in turn and remove the blu-tack/low-tack peel.

8 If you wish to cover a series of bins, you could photocopy the composition on a colour photocopier before sticking it round the bin. Apply a coat of PVA glue to the back of the lining paper and stick it around the bin.

9 If there is a slight overlap at the top edge, trim it neatly using a craft knife.

10 Give the design a coat of varnish and leave to dry.

11 Glue a piece of cord with tassel trim to the rim of the bin. This elegant finish is perfect for covering an untidy edge.

DUMMY BOARD

EMMA WHITFIELD

DUMMY BOARDS are flat, life-sized wooden figures, traditionally painted to resemble people – and sometimes animals. They have their origins in *trompe-l'œil* and were invented in the 16th century by Cornelius Bisschop, who used to place them in doorways or corners to deceive the unwary.

Traditionally, dummy boards were decorated with painted images. With the advent of the photocopier and its enlarging facility, this 20th-century decoupage equivalent is an exciting development, using a photograph of a real cat as its basic image. All you need is a picture of a favourite pet, the use of a colour photocopier, and a few rudimentary woodworking skills.

~

MATERIALS AND EQUIPMENT

- *photograph of cat, enlarged on a colour photocopier*
- *scissors* ● *piece of plywood*
- *soft pencil* ● *D-clamp*
- *fine-bladed saw* ● *fine sandpaper* ● *print fixative*
- *PVA glue* ● *polyurethane varnish* ● *brushes for gluing and varnishing* ● *screw-in rings or brackets, or a triangular section of wood as a stand*

. . . . . .

1 Choose a drawing or photograph from which to make the dummy board. A cat was used here, but other animals can be equally fun to make. The board can be made using a large print or an enlarged photocopy of the image.

2 Cut out the cat using scissors. Keep the shape simple: any narrow pieces, such as a tail, will be difficult to saw and may break off.

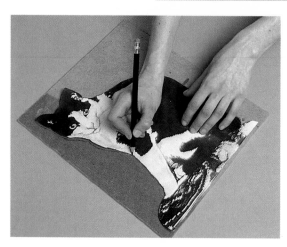

3 Place the cut-out shape on the plywood and draw around it using a soft pencil. Be as accurate as possible, as this will be both the cutting and sticking line.

4 Place the board on a work
surface, and secure with a D-
clamp. Following the pencil line,
saw out the shape. Using fine
sandpaper, sand the edges until
smooth. Brush away any dust from
the surface of the board.

5 Seal the front of the cat image
with print fixative, then cover
the back with glue. Position it very
carefully over the plywood shape
and press firmly into place. If
necessary, carefully trim away any
excess paper.

6 When the glue is dry, paint on a
coat of varnish. Leave to dry
before adding further coats of
varnish. When the varnish is dry,
attach the rings to the back of the
board so it can be hung on a wall,
or secure to a triangular piece of
wood with brackets as a stand.

GOLDEN FLOWER BOWL

MARION ELLIOT

THIS GLASS flower bowl has been decoupaged inside with flowers and butterflies and then given a coat of gold spray paint. The effect is similar to gilding but is only a fraction of the cost, and takes half the time. The old-fashioned double-roses were taken from reproductions of 19th-century American designs and were chosen to complement the roundness of the bowl. For a more oriental look, you could decorate a slender pot or jar in the same way with pictures of lilies, orchids and exotic blooms.

Bowls such as this can be purchased fairly inexpensively from any department store. The decoupaged bowl will not be suitable for holding water, but is perfect for dried flowers.

~

**MATERIALS AND
EQUIPMENT**

● *glass bowl* ● *flower prints*
● *scissors* ● *print fixative*
● *PVA glue* ● *brush for
gluing* ● *gold spray paint*

. . . . . .

1 A plain glass bowl was used for
this project, but any glass
container may be used, including
storage jars. If the container is
painted as well as decoupaged it
should not be used for storing food
unless the paint specifically
indicates that it is non-toxic. (A
round bowl is not the easiest shape
to paint as the paint may run down
the sides of the bowl, so a tapered
bowl is recommended for a
first project.)

2 The roses used for this project
are particularly suitable as they
are already cut into a curved shape
and will follow the surface of the
bowl. Cut out the required images
using small sharp scissors.

3 Spray each piece of the design with a print fixative. This will help to prevent the colours fading or yellowing with age.

4 Cover the front of the pieces to be decoupaged with PVA glue. (The image will appear through the glass, with the glue transparent when dry.) Stick each piece of the design in position on the inside of the bowl, pressing hard to make sure it is properly stuck.

5 When all the components are dry, spray the gold paint on the inside of the bowl, one section at a time to stop the paint from running down the sides and leaving streaks.

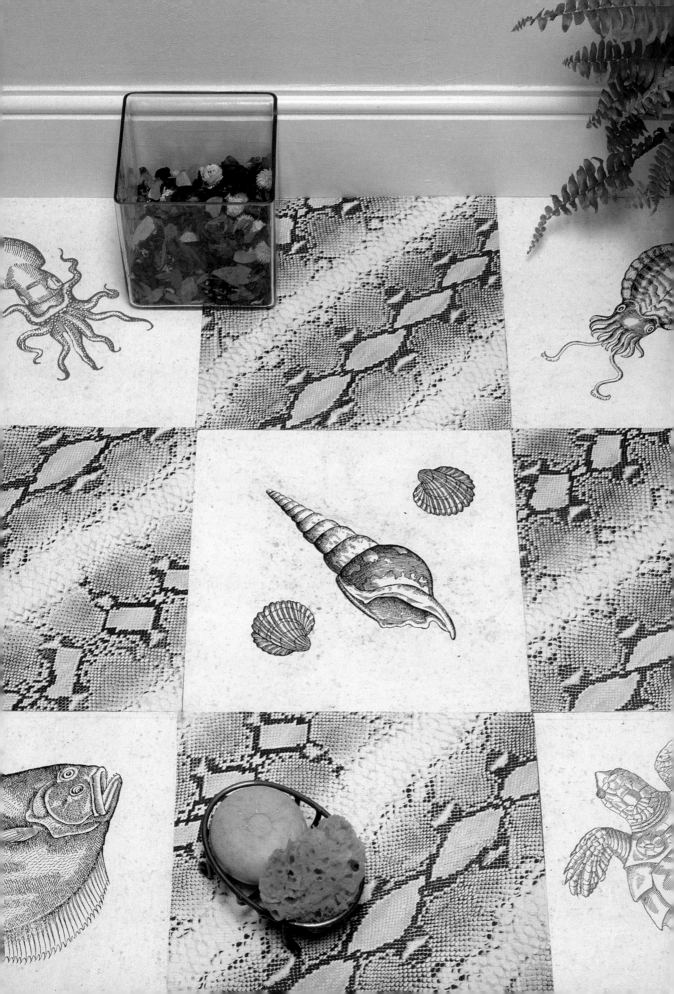

BATHROOM TILES

MARION ELLIOT

THESE EYE-CATCHING tiles started life as ordinary cork floor tiles. They were painted and decoupaged and then given many coats of varnish to make them hardwearing and waterproof.

Snakeskin-printed paper and images from an ancient book on biology create a sea theme perfect for a bathroom, but different designs can be chosen to suit other rooms in the house. Kitchen tiles could be decorated with botanical prints of herbs, fruits and vegetables, for example.

Some of the images used here were photocopied in colour, but hand-tinted black and white prints could be used as well.

~

MATERIALS AND EQUIPMENT

- *cork floor tiles* • *white emulsion paint* • *brushes for painting and gluing*
- *enlarged photocopies from biological book* • *print fixative*
- *scissors* • *snakeskin-printed wrapping paper* • *PVA glue*
- *tile adhesive*

. . . . . .

1 Measure the floor area carefully to ensure you buy enough cork floor tiles to cover the area required.

2 Paint each tile individually with white emulsion paint. If the paint is streaked when dry, add another coat and even a third if necessary.

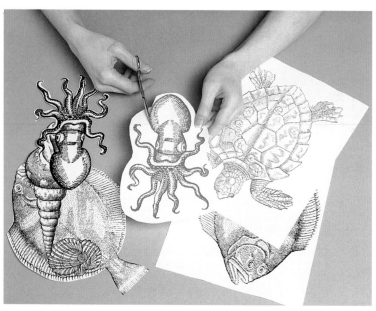

3 Photocopy and enlarge the images you wish to use in the centre of the tiles. Cut out each image, using fine scissors for the details. Seal with a print fixative.

4 Cut out the snakeskin-printed wrapping paper on the cross so that the pattern lies on the diagonal. Cut enough squares to cover half of the tiles. Seal with a print fixative.

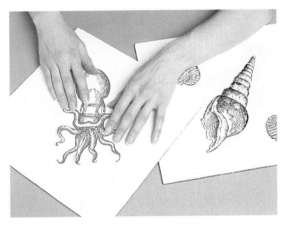

5 Using the PVA glue, stick the snakeskin-printed paper on to the tiles. Press down firmly.

6 Arrange the sea images on the white tiles and glue them into position on the diagonal.

7 Give each tile a coat of diluted PVA to varnish. Leave to dry and then repeat the process seven more times to ensure the tiles are waterproof. Use tile adhesive to stick them to the floor in the required pattern.

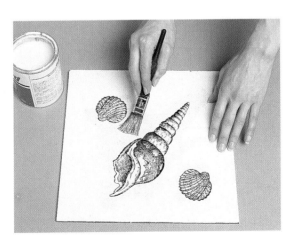

MUSIC CUPBOARD

JOSEPHINE WHITFIELD

An old junk shop find is transformed into a music cupboard by the use of paint, crackle varnish, tea-aged sheets of music, and some ingenuity. It is often hard to see the potential in old pieces of furniture: this cupboard was originally brown, with an ugly formica top and bakelite handle.

Crackle varnish rubbed with oil paint was used to create a finish in keeping with the old sheet music decorating the sides. Prints of musical instruments add depth to the composition and complete the theme.

~

MATERIALS AND EQUIPMENT

- *old cupboard* • *white spirit*
- *white emulsion paint*
- *brushes for painting, varnishing and gluing*
- *antique varnish* • *crackle varnish* • *burnt umber or black oil paint* • *rag* • *sheet music and photocopies of music prints* • *used tea bag*
- *print fixative* • *scissors*
- *PVA glue* • *spray adhesive (optional)*

· · · · · ·

1 An old piece of furniture can seem beyond hope at first, but once painted and decoupaged, it will be transformed. This cupboard's formica top is too firmly stuck down to be removed, so it is better to decorate it. The handle on the door will be replaced with a brass knob more in keeping with the new, decoupaged look.

2 Clean the cupboard with white spirit to prevent any problems with adhesion and to give a clean, dust-free surface on which to work.

3 Paint the outside of the cupboard with a sealing coat of white emulsion paint. When it is dry paint the edge of the door and the inside of the cupboard. Leave to dry thoroughly.

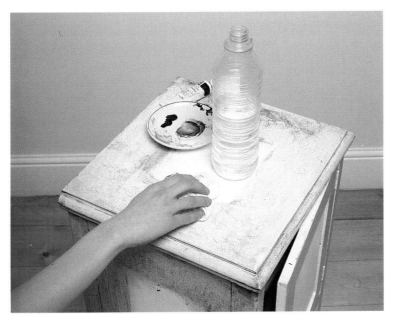

4 Apply antique varnish and leave until still sticky but not wet. Apply crackle varnish on top of the antique varnish, and leave until cracks appear. If cracks do not appear after an hour, the process may be speeded up by applying heat from a hair dryer. When the process is complete and the cracking is dry, rub some oil paint into the cracks with a rag.

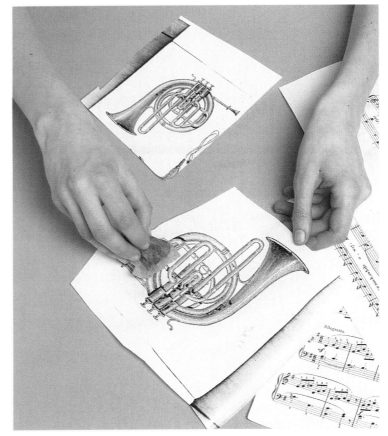

5 Rub the sheet music paper and the photocopies or prints of musical instruments with a cold, wet tea bag to produce a browny-yellow 'aged' look. Leave to dry. If the paper crinkles too much, flatten gently with a cool iron. Seal the papers with a print fixative.

6 Stick the sheets of music on to the top and the front of the cupboard using PVA glue. Press down well to ensure there are no bumps or creases.

7 Cut out the details of musical instruments, seal with a print fixative and stick down using a spray adhesive or PVA glue.

8 Apply a coating of PVA glue as a sealant over the entire cupboard and leave to dry.

SUPPLIERS

GENERAL TRADING COMPANY LTD, 144 Sloane Street, London SW1X 9BL, UK. Tel: 071 730 0411 (Decorated furniture)

GLOBAL VILLAGE, 17 St James Street, South Petherton, Somerset TA13 5BS, UK. Tel: 0460 41166 (Mail order items)

PANDURO HOBBY LTD, West Way House, Transport Avenue, Brentford, Middlesex TW8 9HF, UK. Tel: 081 847 6161 (Hat boxes by mail order)

HAWKIN & CO., Saint Margaret, Harleston, Norfolk IP20 0PJ, UK. Tel: 0986 82536 (Decoupage scraps by mail order)

ORNAMENTA, PO Box 784, London SW7 2TG, UK. Tel: 071 584 3857 (Cherubs, border designs and print room decorations)

MAMELOK PRESS LTD, Northern Way, Bury St Edmunds, Suffolk IP32 6NJ, UK. Tel: 0284 762291 (Specialist scrap printers)

THE DOVER BOOKSHOP, 18 Earlham Street, London WC2H 9LN, UK. Tel: 071 836 2111 (Specialists in books of scraps and borders)

DOVER PUBLICATIONS INC, 31 East 2nd Street, Mineola, NY 11501, USA. Tel: 212 255 3755

PAPER E. CLIPS, 20 Maud Street, Suite 307, Toronto, Ontario M5Y 2M5, Canada. Tel: 416 941 9075 (Greetings cards and scraps)

ROSENHAIN, LIPMANN & PEERS PTY, 147 Burnley Street, Richmond, Melbourne, Victoria 3121, Australia. Tel: 03 428 1485 (Paper products and scraps)

THE PARTNERS, St Martins Stationery, 5 Austin-Kirk Lane, Christchurch 2, New Zealand. (Greetings cards, scraps and paper products)

The following artists would be pleased to accept commissions for decoupage work:

EMMA WHITFIELD Tel: 081 674 5220

JOSEPHINE WHITFIELD Tel: 071 733 0668

MARION ELLIOT, 91 Huddlestone Road, London N7 0AE, UK. Tel: 071 831 6212

JULIETTE PIERCE, Cross Street Studios, 14 Cross Street, Hove, Sussex BN3 1AJ, UK. Tel: 0273 725321

STEVE WRIGHT, 45 Melbourne Grove, London SE22 8RG, UK. Tel: 081 299 3164

DENISE THOMAS, Flat 1, 36 Lingfield Road, London SW19 4PZ, UK. Tel: 081 946 8397

GERRY COPP, School Cottage, Aisthorpe, Lincoln LN1 2SG, UK. Tel: 0522 730218

NICOLA WINGATE SAUL, 47 Morton Terrace, London SW1V 2NS, UK. Tel: 071 821 1577 (*Print room specialist*)

ANGELA SHAW, Flexford House, Hog's Back, Guildford, Surrey GU3 2JP, UK. Tel: 0483 810223

KATHY WEBSTER & ROSY BURMAN, Paper Roses, 24 Milverton Terrace, Leamington Spa CV32 5BA, UK. Tel; 0926 312980

INDEX

A

Acrylic paint, 11
Artists' oils, 11

B

Basic techniques, 14–15
Basket, waste-paper, 73–77
Bathroom tiles, 87–89
Biedermeier style, 9
Bowl, golden flower, 83–85
Box,
    hat, 37–39
    heart, 33–35
    jewellery, 69–71
Braque, Georges, 9
Brushes, 12
Byron, Lord, 9

C

Celestial clock, 57–59
Chair, kitchen, 47–49
Circus frieze, 65–67
Cleaning materials, 11
Collage, 9
Composition,
    design and, 14
Cupboard, music, 91–94
Cutting, 15

D

Decoupage,
    items to, 10
    tin, 61–63
Design and composition, 14
Dressing room screen, 41–45
Duer, Caroline, 9
Dummy board, 79–81

E

Elliot, Marion, 61, 65, 69, 83,
    87
Emulsion, 11
Enamel, 11
Equipment,
    materials and, 10–13

F

Floral mirror, 51–55
Frieze, circus, 65–67

G

Gallery, 17–25
Gesso, acrylic, 11
Glues, 12
Golden flower bowl, 83–85

H

Hat box, 37–39
Heart boxes, 33–35

J

Japanning, 7
Jewellery box, 69–71

K

Kitchen chair, 47–49

L

Louis XIV, 7

M

Materials and equipment, 10
Matt/flat wood paints, 11
Metal,
    preparing new, 15
    preparing old, 15
Mirror, floral, 51–55
Music cupboard, 91–94

P

Paints, 11
Picasso, Pablo, 9
Polishing,
    varnishing and, 15
Priming, 15
Print,
    fixatives, 10
    sealers, 10
Printed material, 10
Prints,
    sealing paper, 14
    thinning thick, 14

Q

Queen Victoria, 9

S

Screen, dressing room, 41–45
Shellac, 10
Spray paint, 11
Sticking, 15
Suppliers, 95
Surfaces, preparing, 15

T

Techniques,
    cutting, 15
    design and composition, 14
    paper prints, sealing, 14
    priming, 15
    sticking, 15
    surfaces, preparing, 15
    thick prints, thinning, 14
    varnishing and polishing, 15
Tiles, bathroom, 87–89
Tin, decoupage, 61–63
Tray, Victorian, 27–31

U

Undercoat, 11

V

Varnishes, 11
Varnishing and polishing, 15
Victorian tray, 27–31

W

Walpole, Horace, 8
Waste-paper basket, 73–77
Whitfield, Emma, 27, 33, 37,
    41, 79
Whitfield, Josephine, 47, 51, 57,
    73, 91
Wood,
    paints, matt/flat, 11
    preparing painted, 15